BERMAGUI ART BOOK

Drawn memories of Bermagui by Joel Tarling

For Mum and Dad

www.joeltarling.com

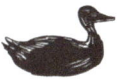 I would like to acknowledge The Djiringanj Clan of the Yuin Nation who have been the custodians of this country from the Shoalhaven River at Nowra and down the coast into Mallacoota Lake at the border of Victoria for 40,000 to 50,000 years.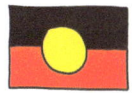

About this book:

In the 80's I grew up in Bermagui. My mum, dad, big sister Amber and I lived at Barragga Bay, in a spotted gum forest dotted with burrawongs. This was where my parents built our family home, "Apocalypse Cottage". At the age of 10, we moved away to Sydney. Over the years, I would regularly return south to see family friends. When I was 20, I was very fortunate to live in Bermagui again for a month, with a family friend, Clayton. Bermagui has always felt like my home. These artworks are a celebration of my feelings of this special part of the world. I hope it captures what others feel about this amazing place, too.

To create these works, I had to juggle my freelance graphic designer/ illustration jobs and my responsibilities as primary carer to our child. It's hard to find time for anything creative, but with the encouragement of my wife Bec, we worked out a way for me to fit my creative work into our lives. I moved my studio area into the dining room, so I could draw at any moment while still being available to our daughter. The moments in between breakfast and the school run have yielded 18 new artworks within a few months. Which became the body of work for a solo exhibition called 'Going Coastal' at the Bermagui Gelati Clinic, Bermagui fisherman's wharf in 2018.

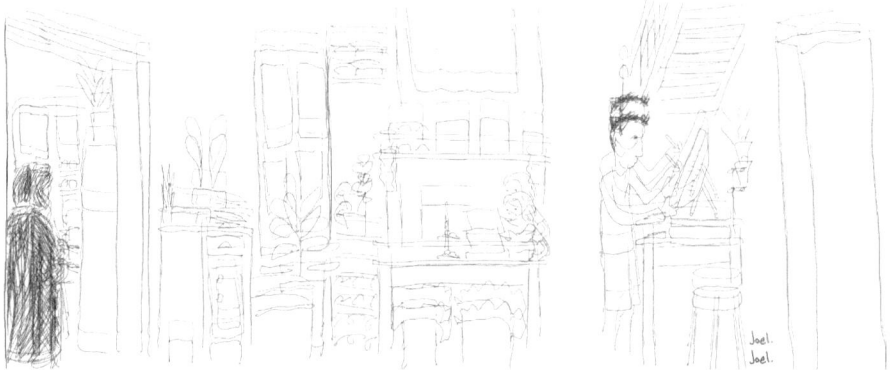

Drawing from memory became a powerful tool, too. Every picture except the Gulga, Wallaga Lake drawing* is completely from memory. I discovered that drawing from memory, I could hit the right emotional tone of my feelings of these people and places. I also loved the freedom of being able to work anywhere, because my only reference was coming from my head all I needed to get it down was pencil, pen and paper.

*The Gulga, Wallaga Lake drawing was created by referring to an actual sketch drawn of the bridge, sitting on a piece of driftwood at the location three years ago.

Special thanks: Bec Plumbe, Liberty Tarling, Amber Tarling, Zoe Tarling, Kate Broadhurst, Allan Broadhurst, Clayton Simms, Matt Craig, Rickie Swain, Glenn Smith, Alberto Cementon, Francesca Cementon, Tim Burke, Jazz Williams and Warren Foster Snr.

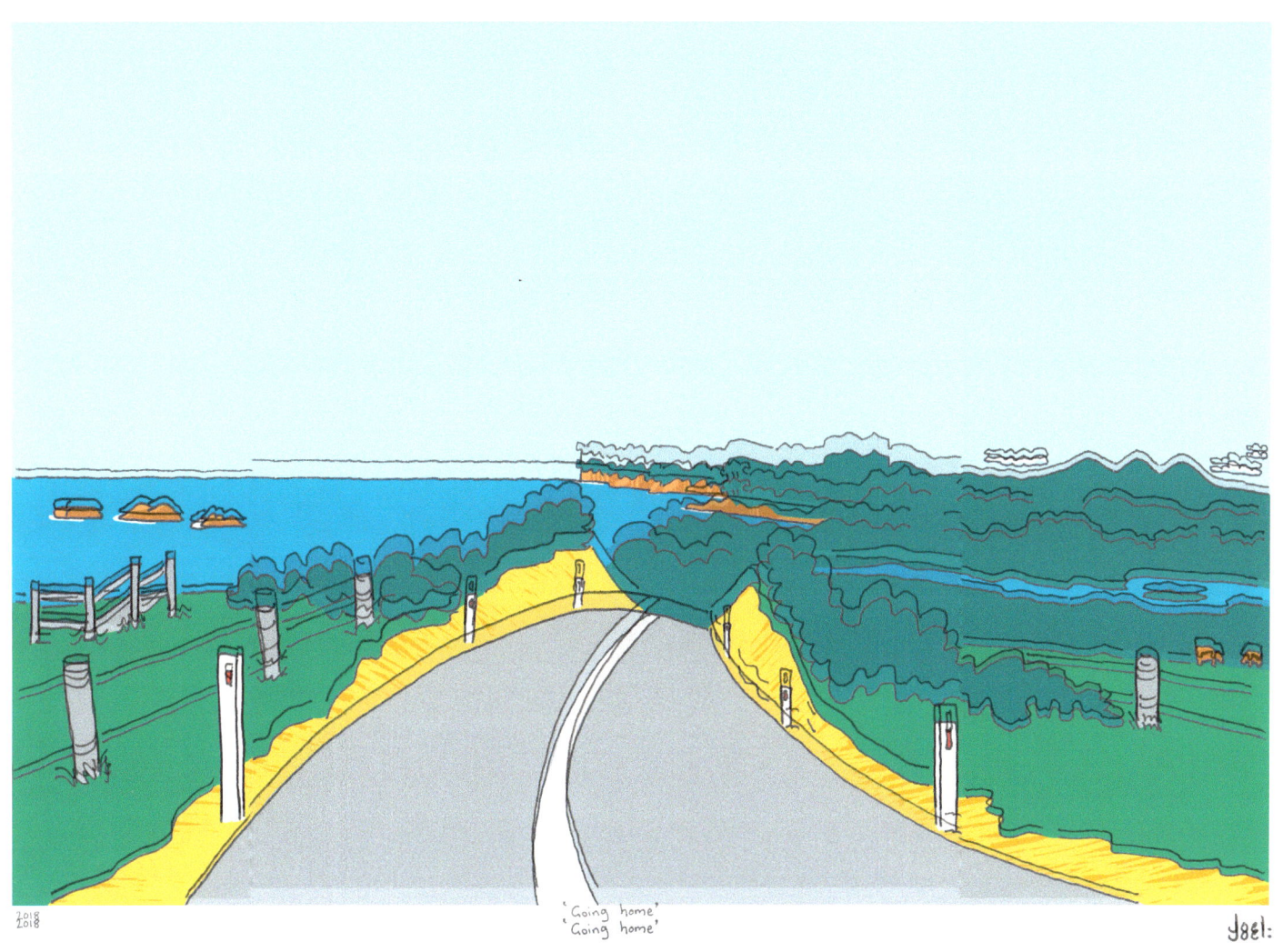

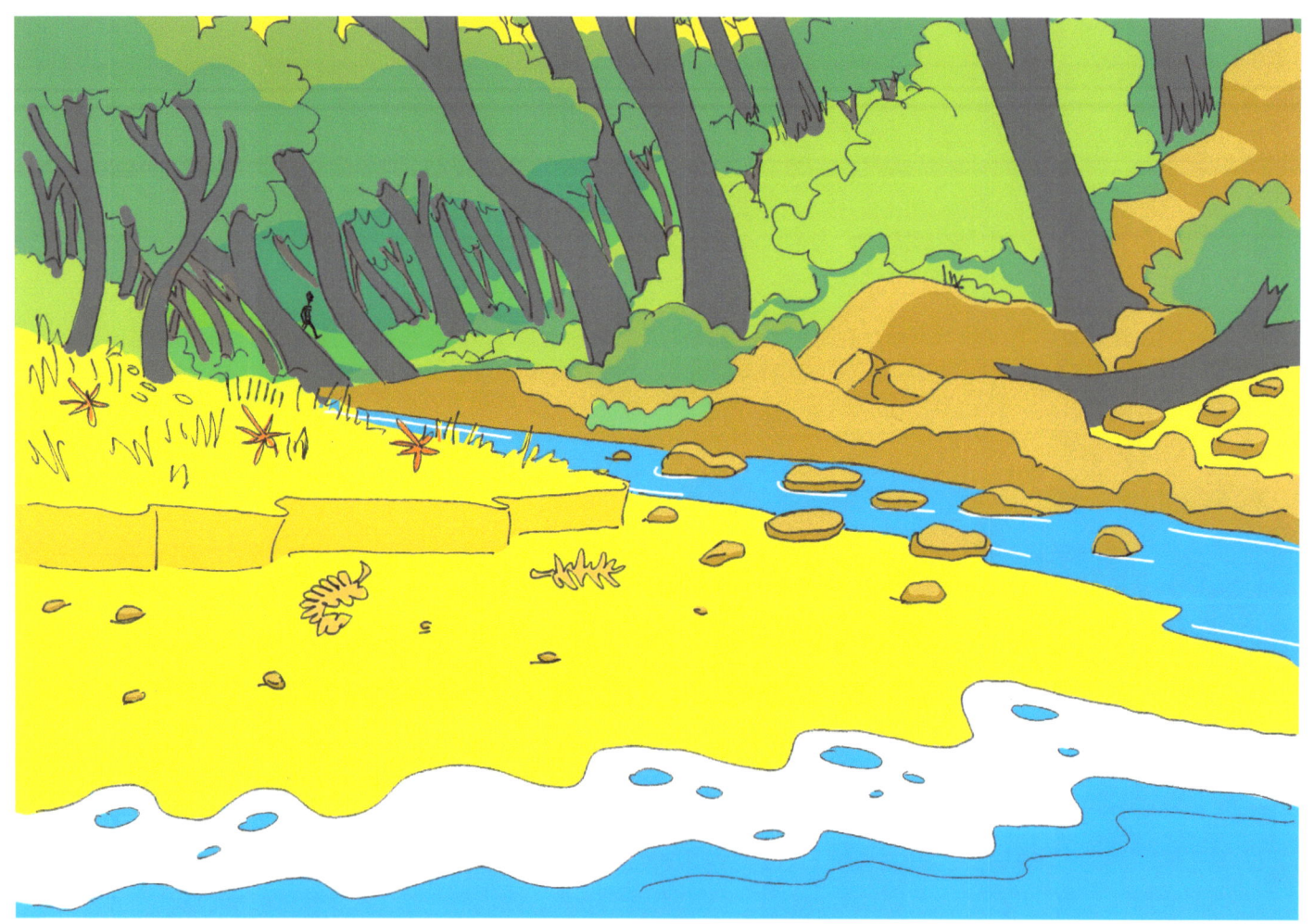

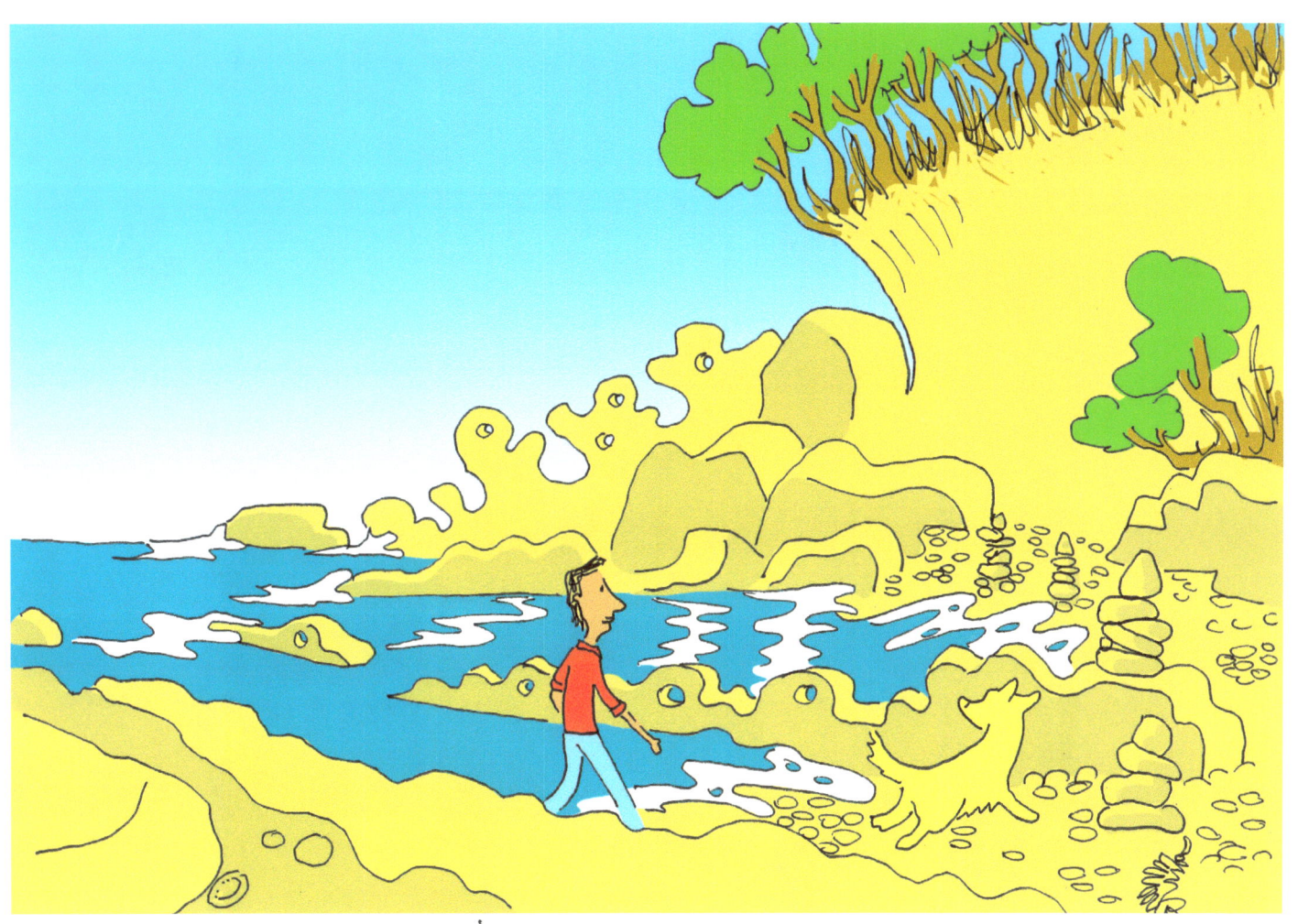

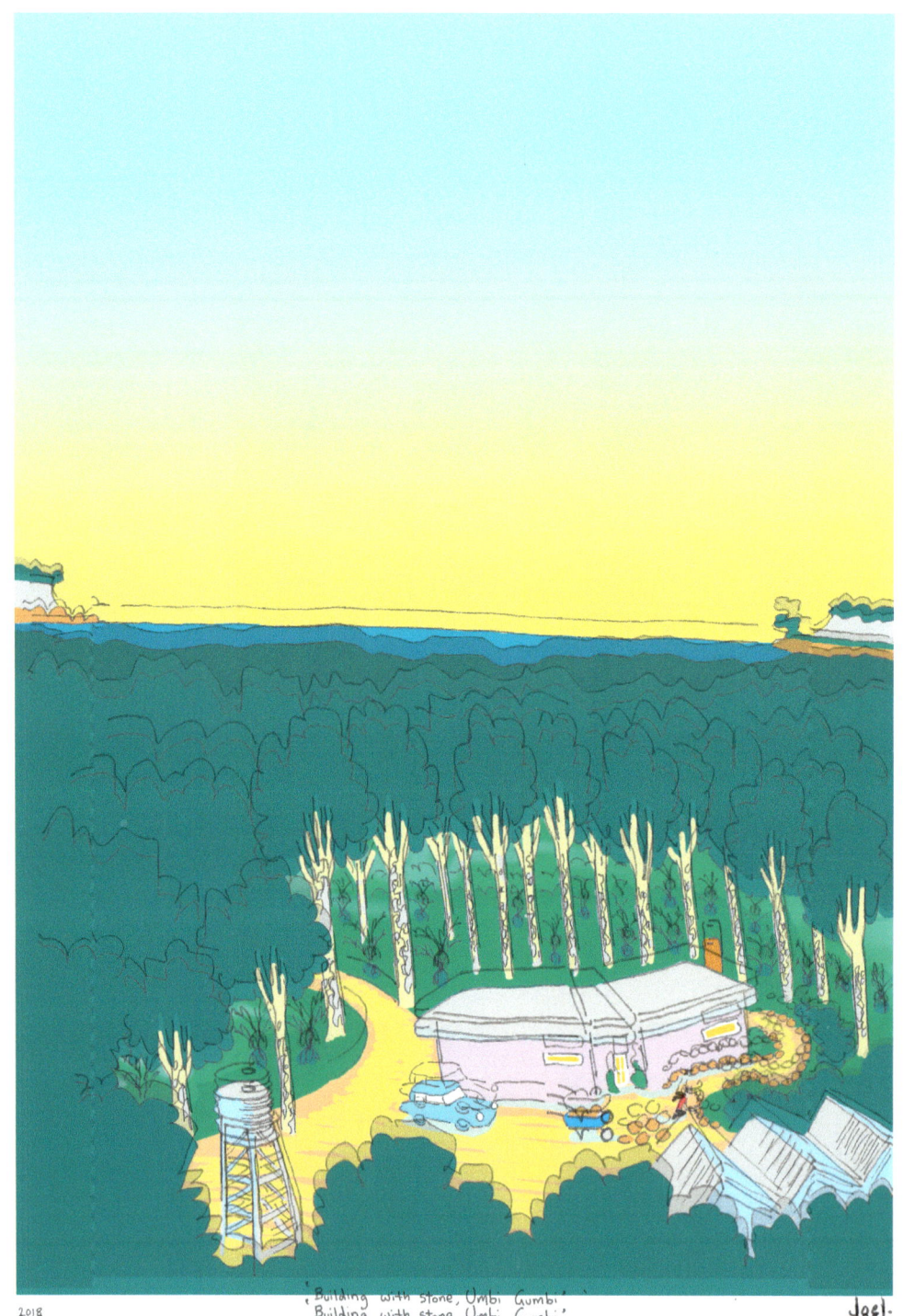

'Building with stone, Umbi Gumbi'

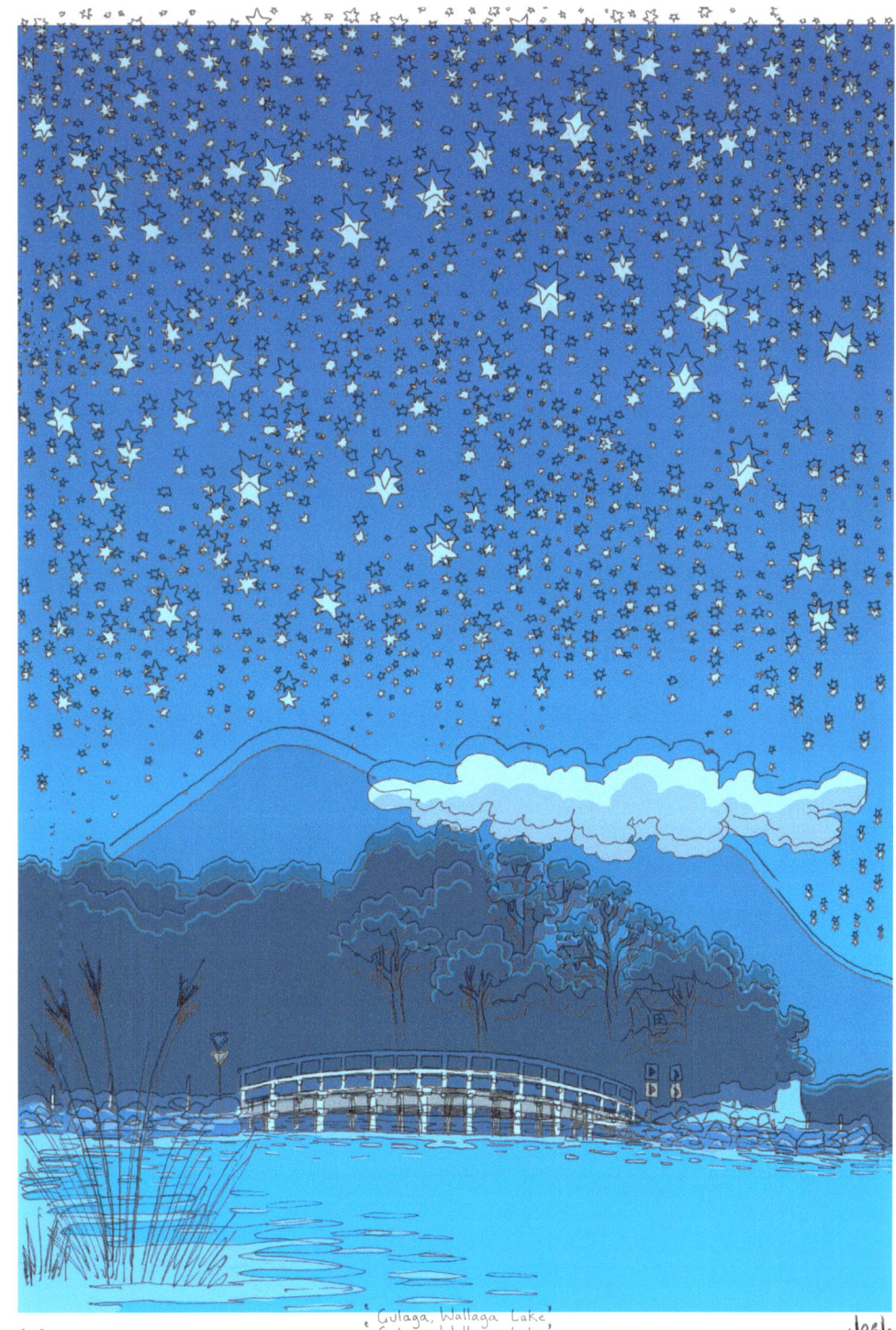

'Gulaga, Wallaga Lake'

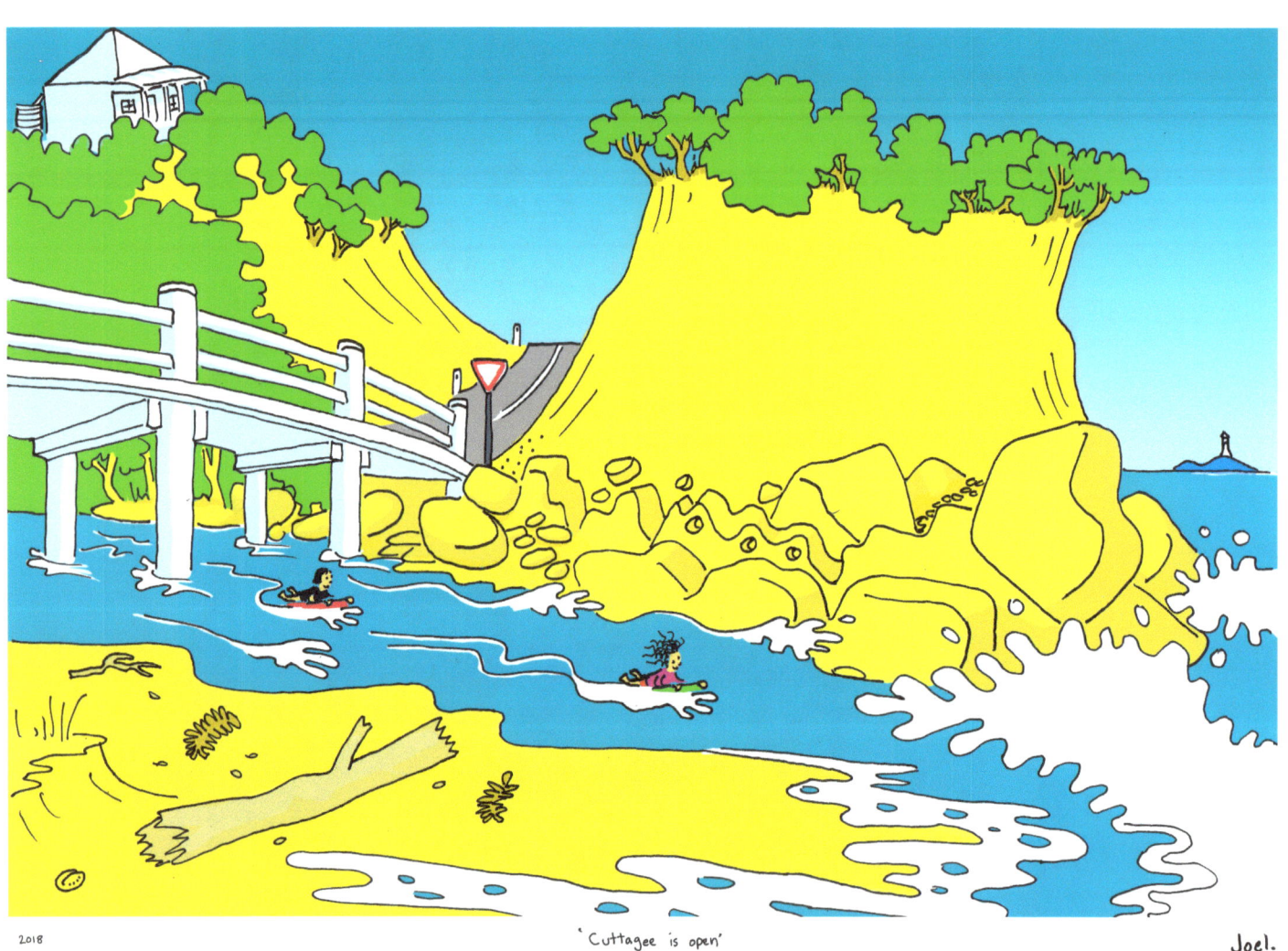

'Cuttagee is open'

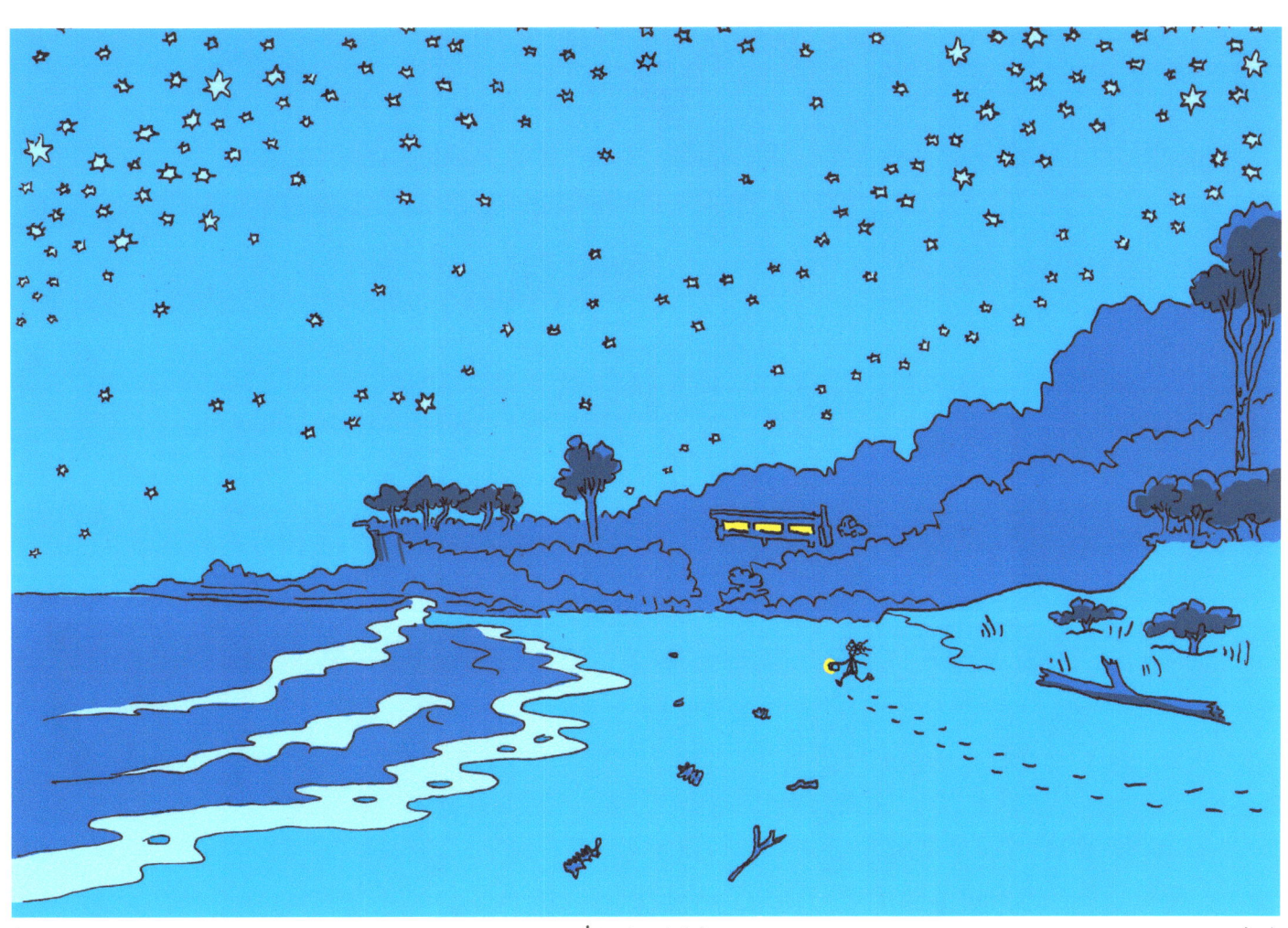

2018   'Getting help'   Joel.

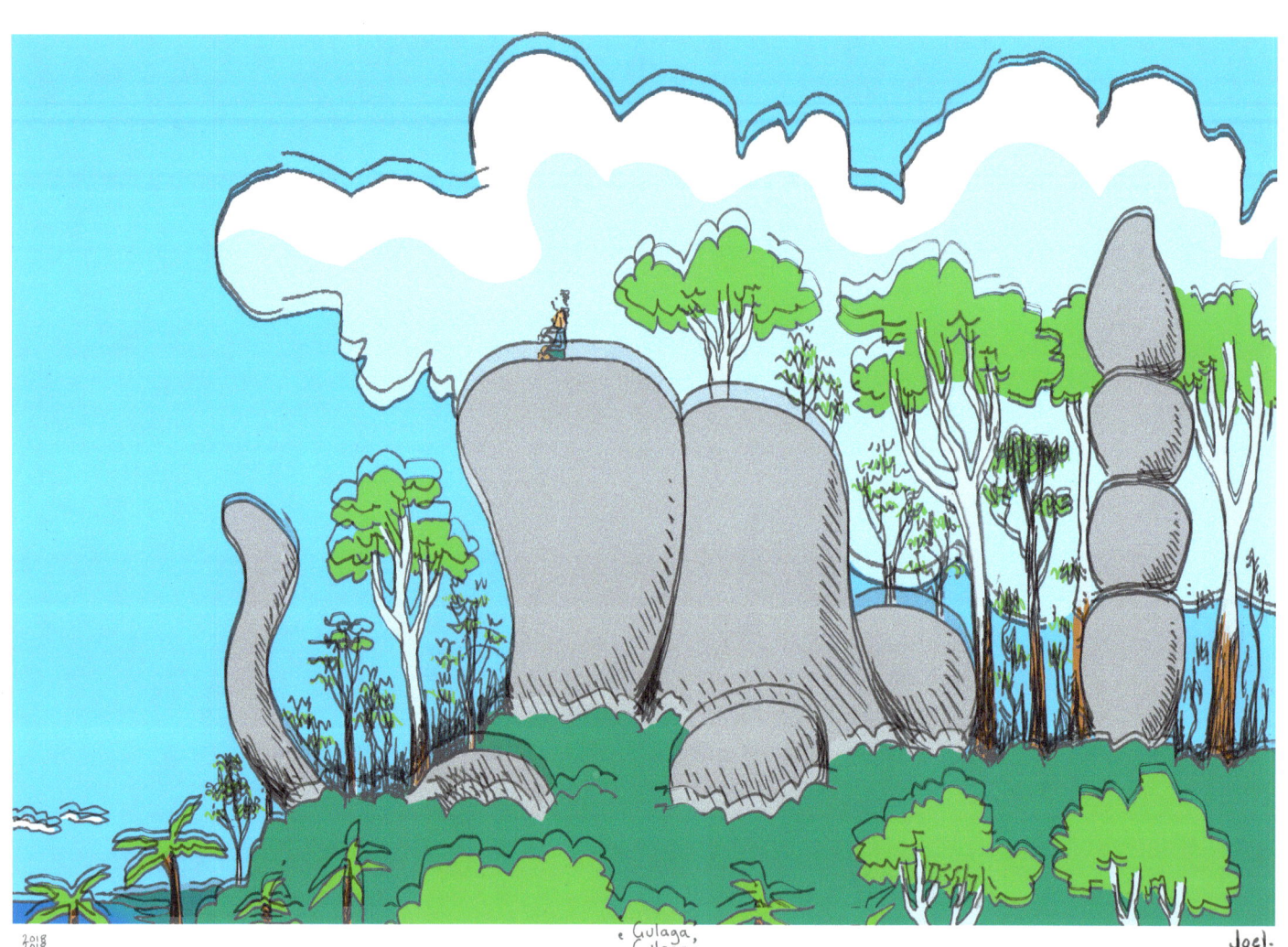

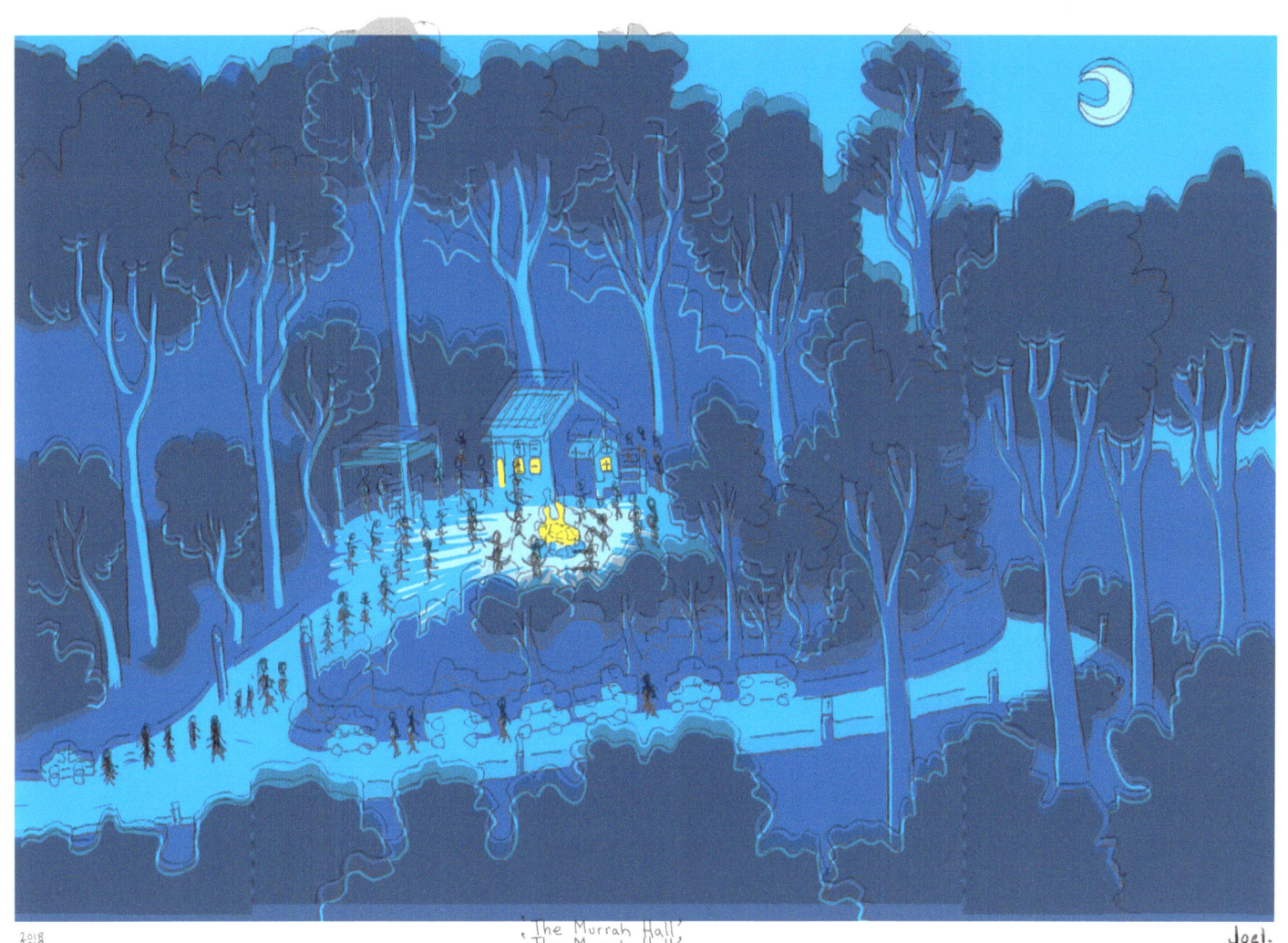

'The Murrah Hall'

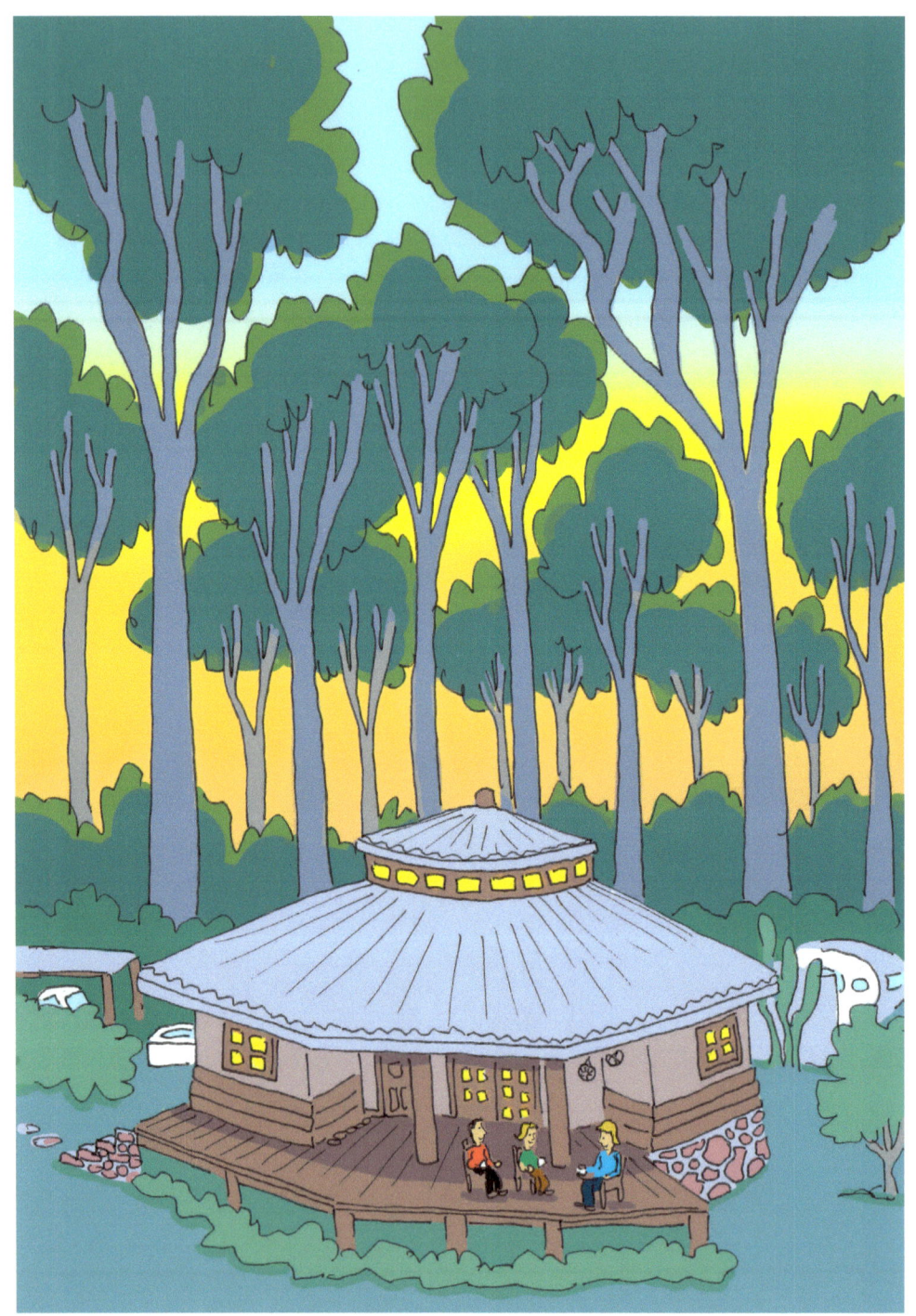

'Talking with Allan'

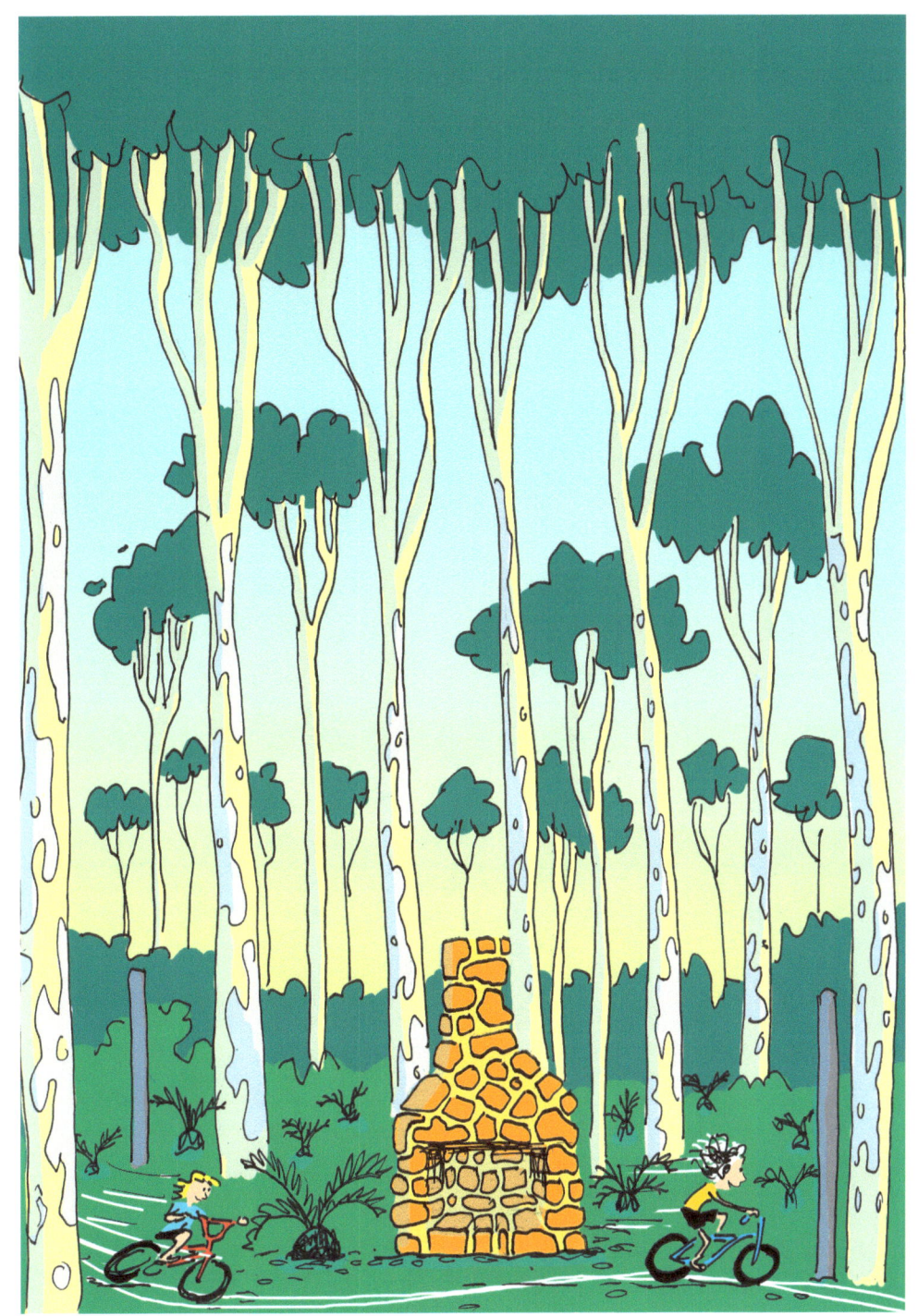

"The racetrack, Burrawong Place"

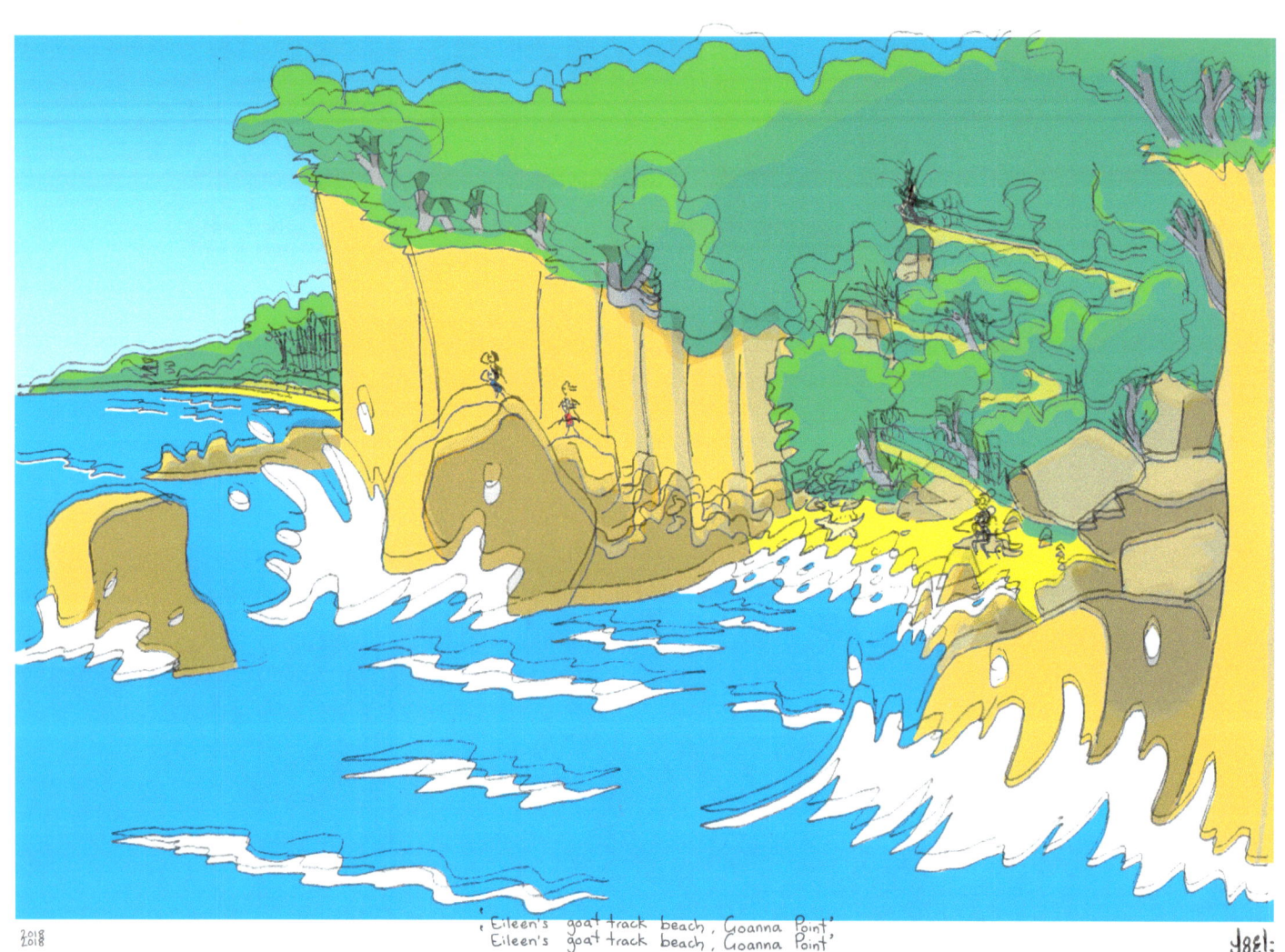

'Eileen's goat track beach, Goanna Point'

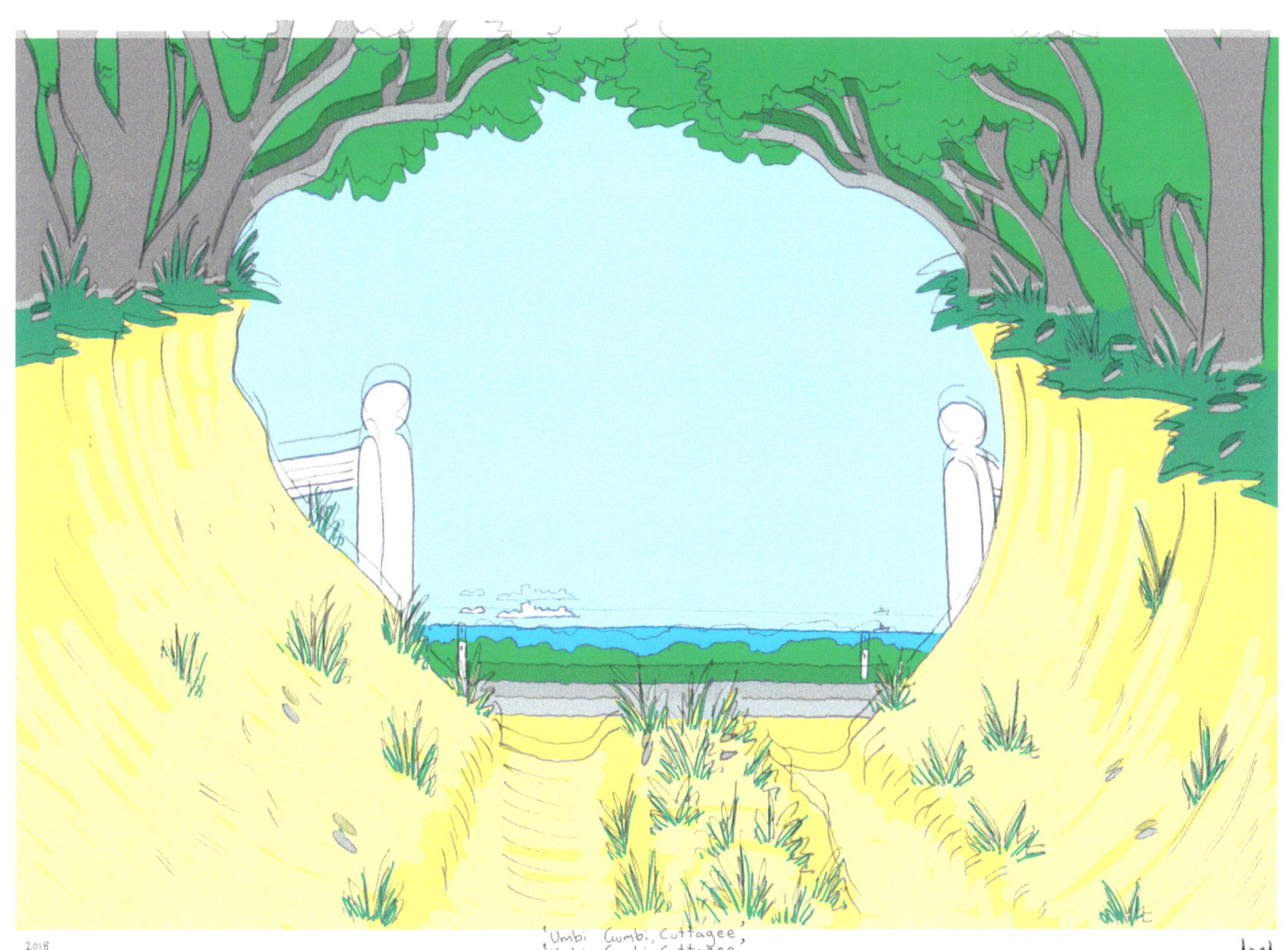

2018/2018 · 'Umbi Gumbi, Cuttagee, Umbi Gumbi, Cuttagee' · yael:

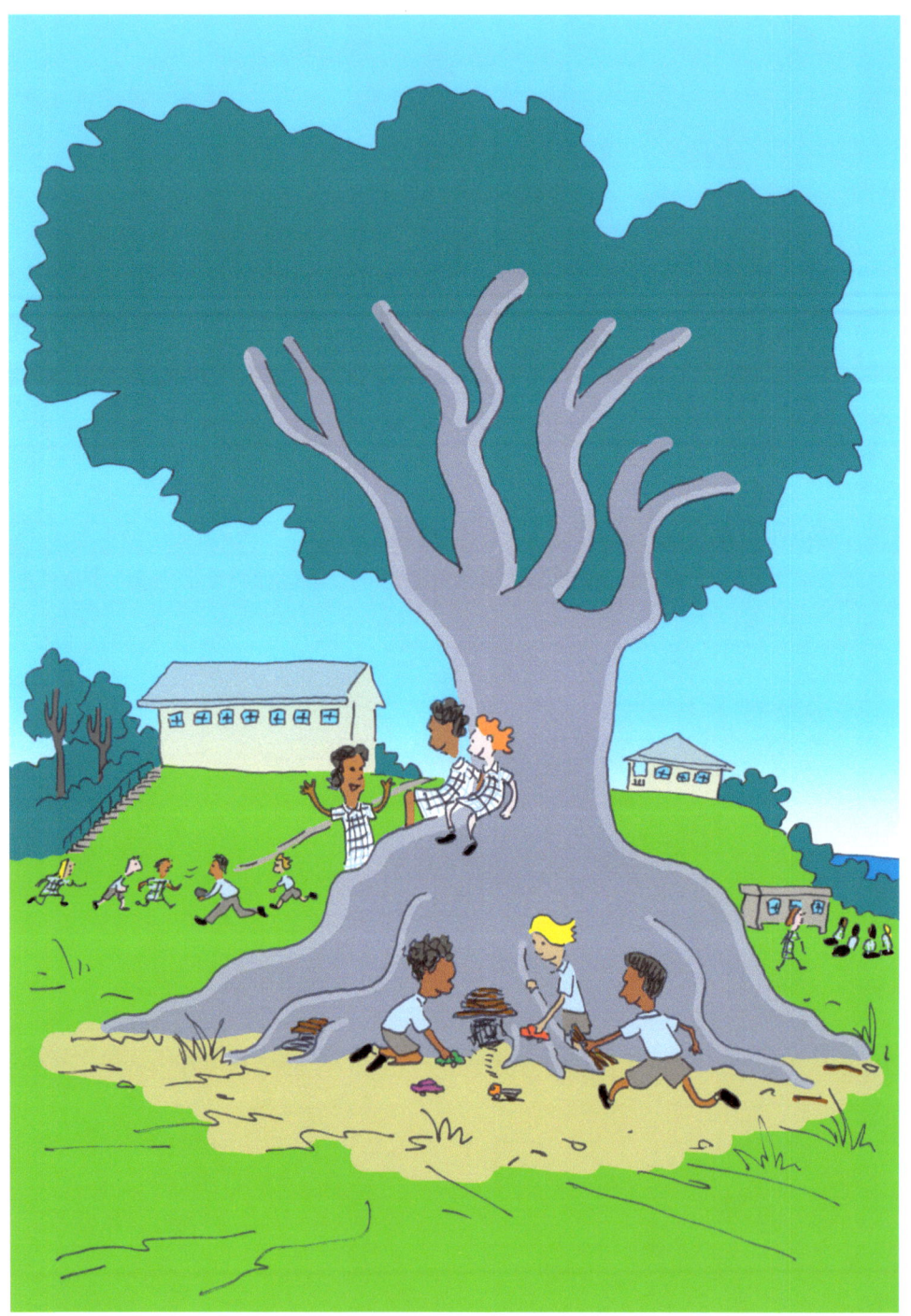

2018   'The big tree, Bermagui Public school'   Joel.

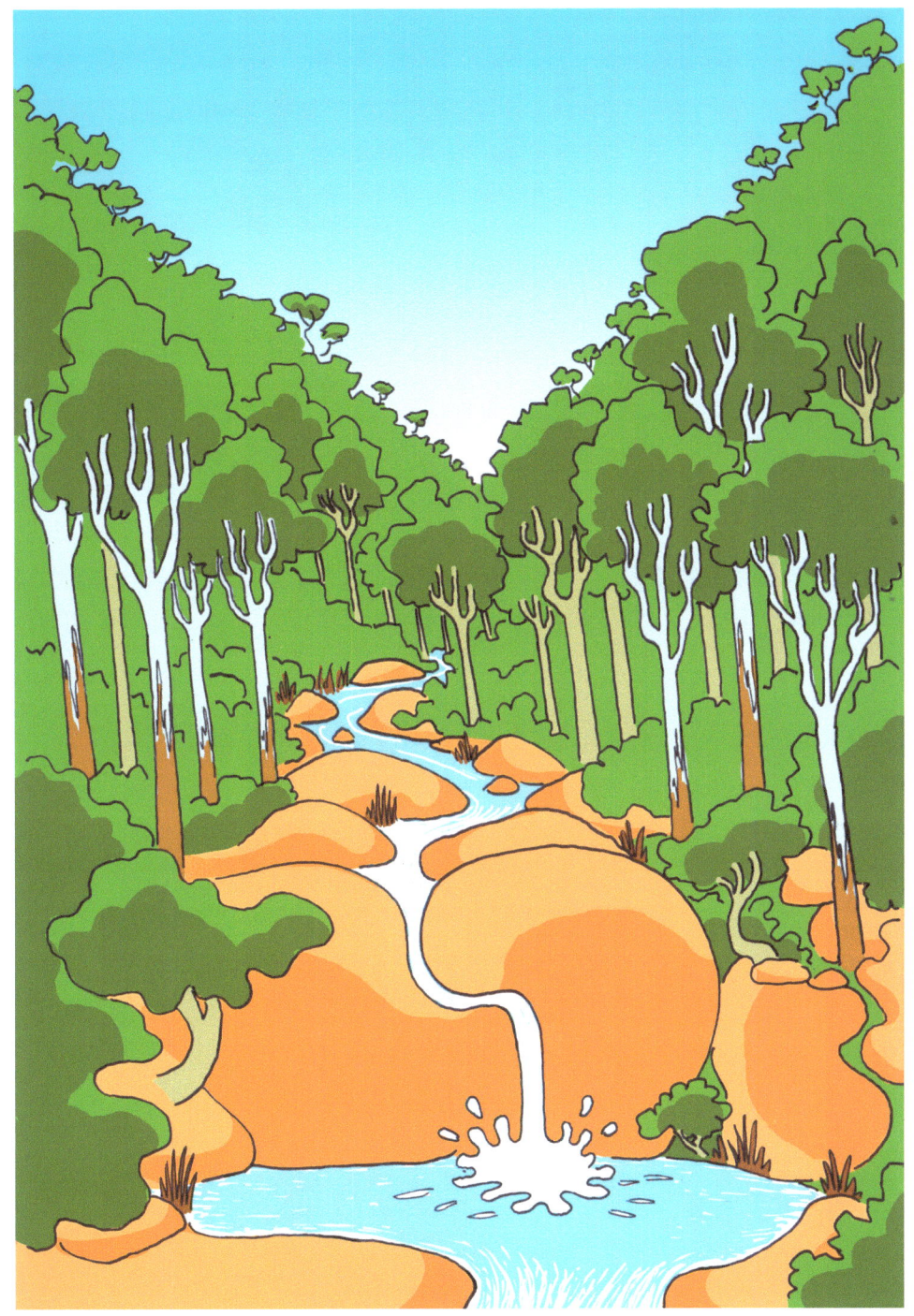

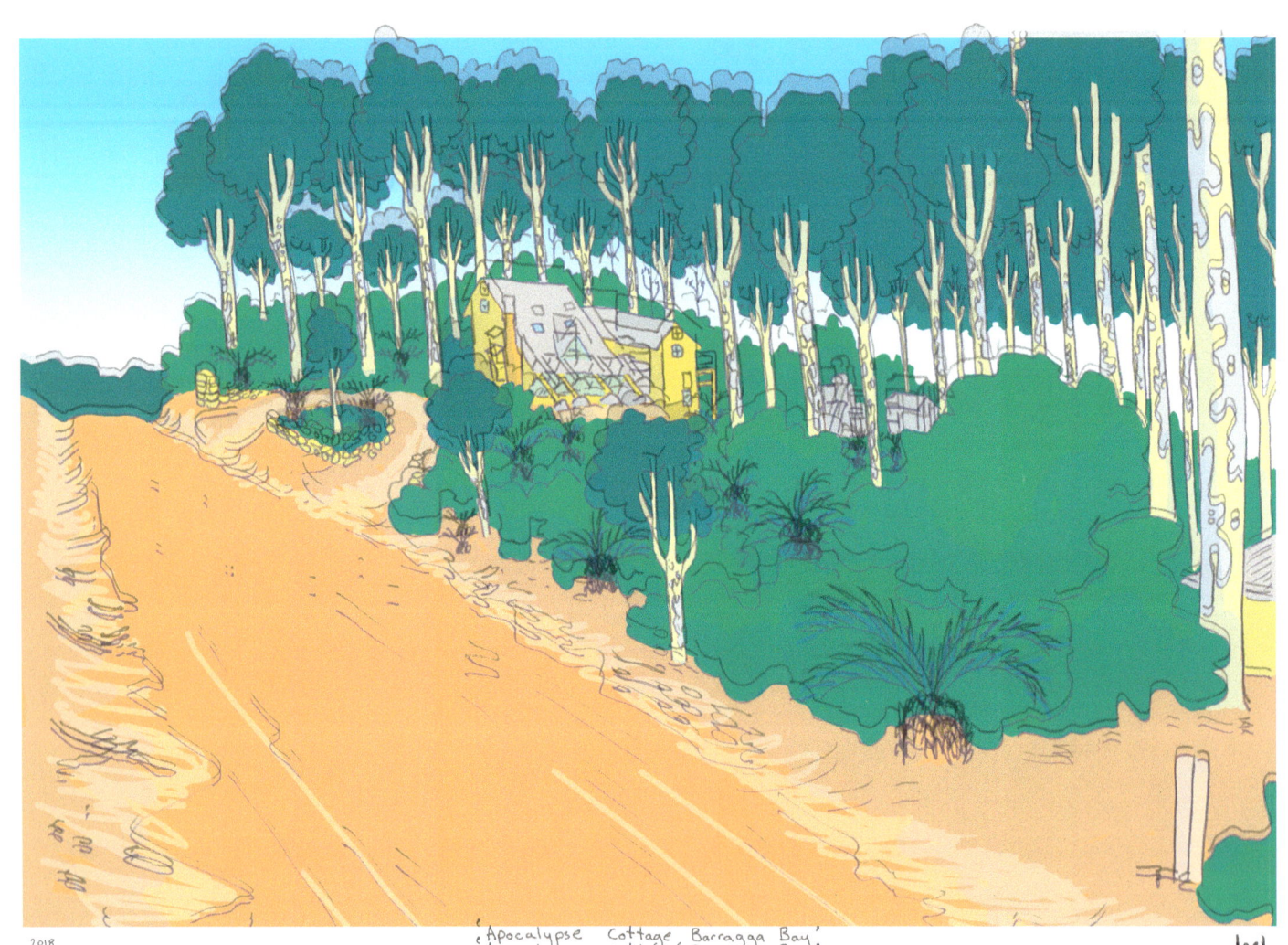

'Apocalypse Cottage, Barragga Bay'

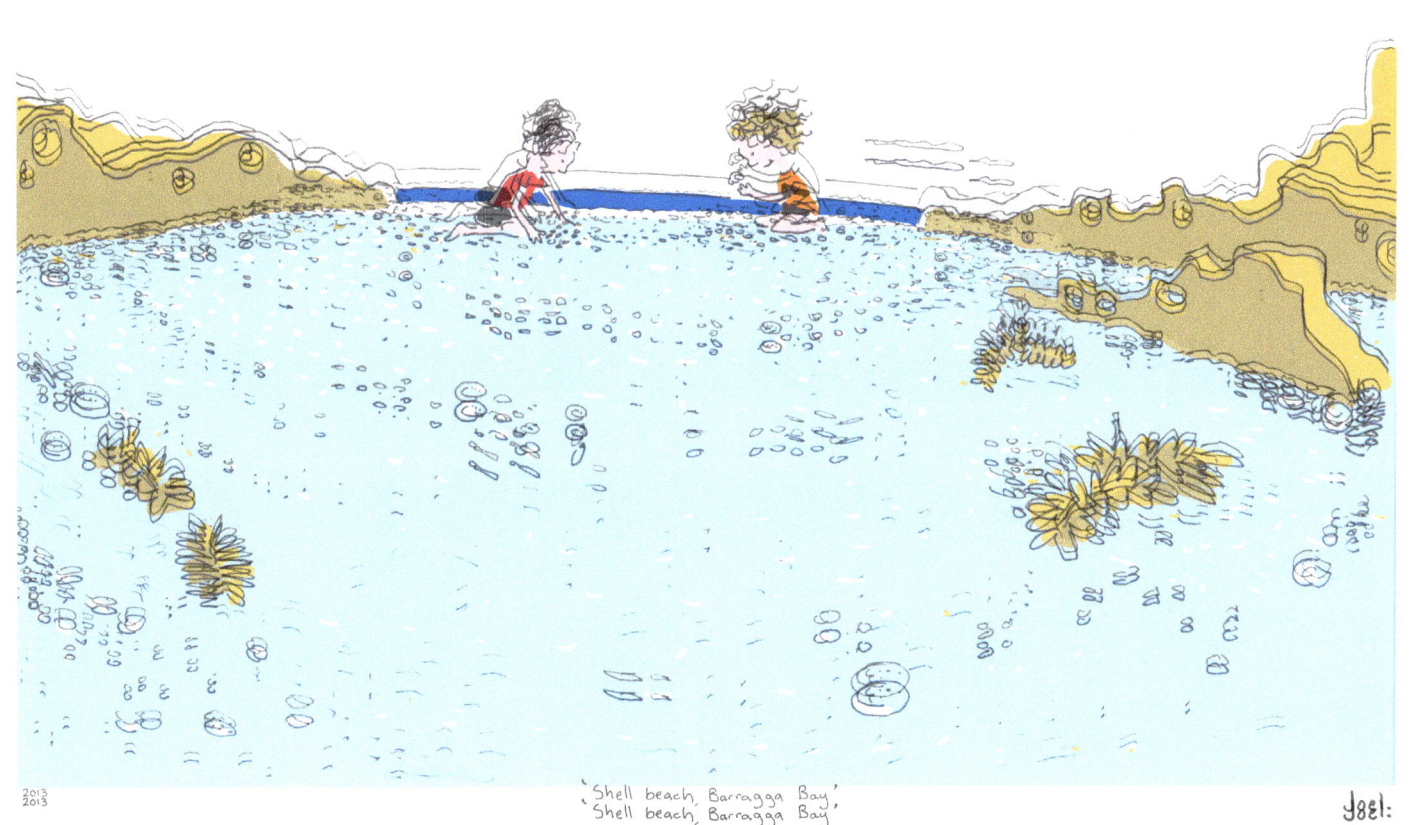

'Shell beach, Barragga Bay'

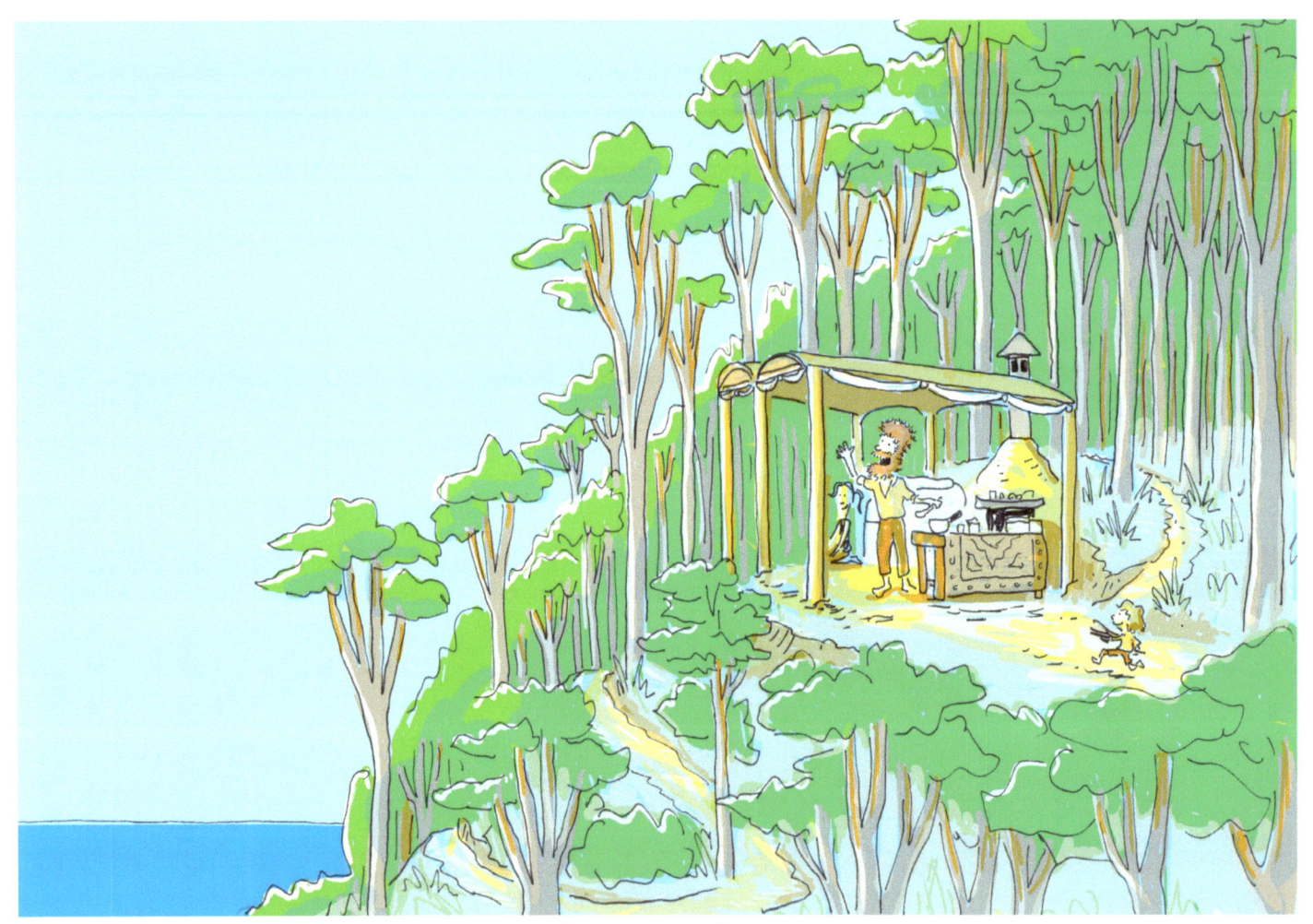

'Wes Stacey's home'

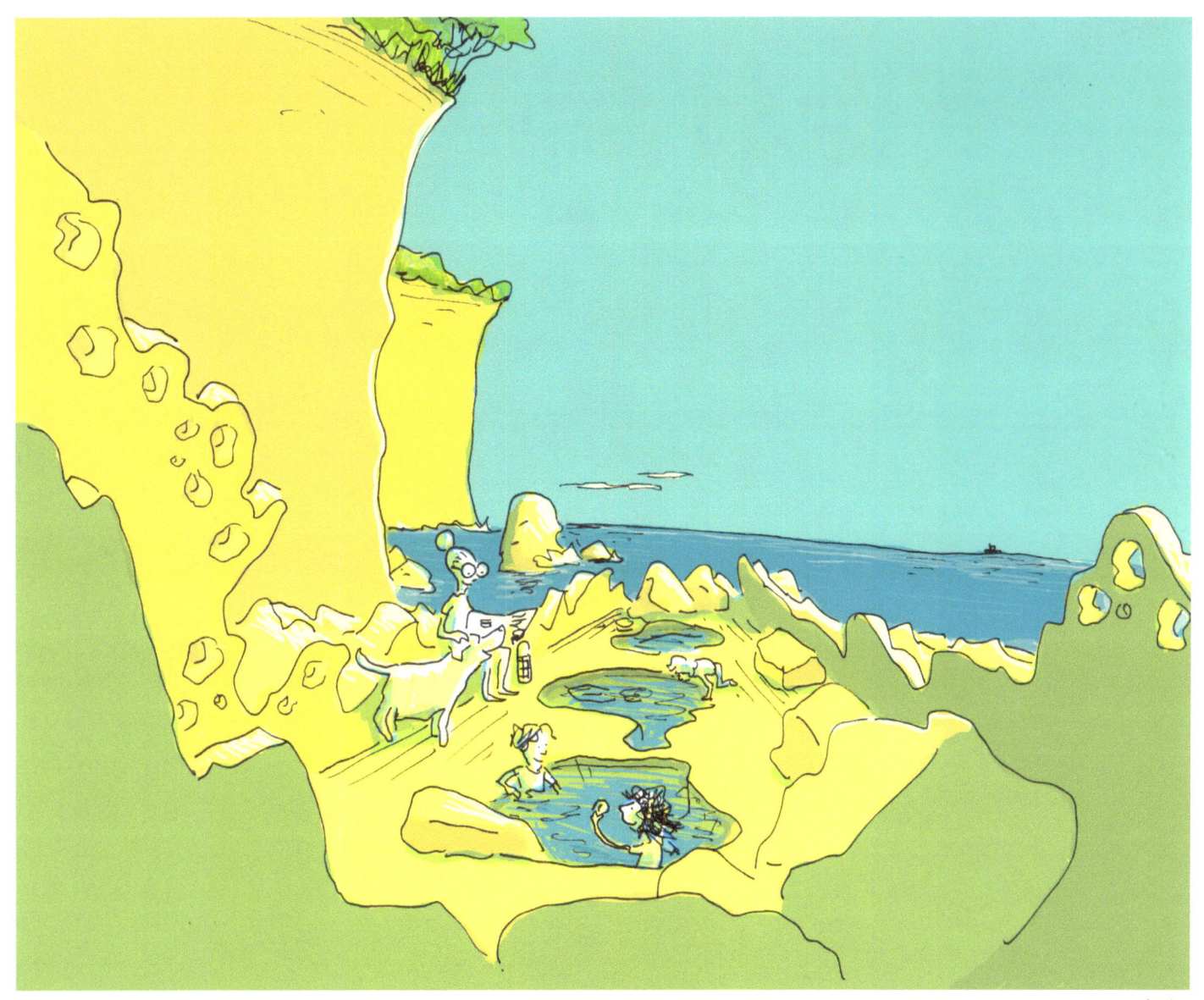

'Rockpools, Barragga Bay'

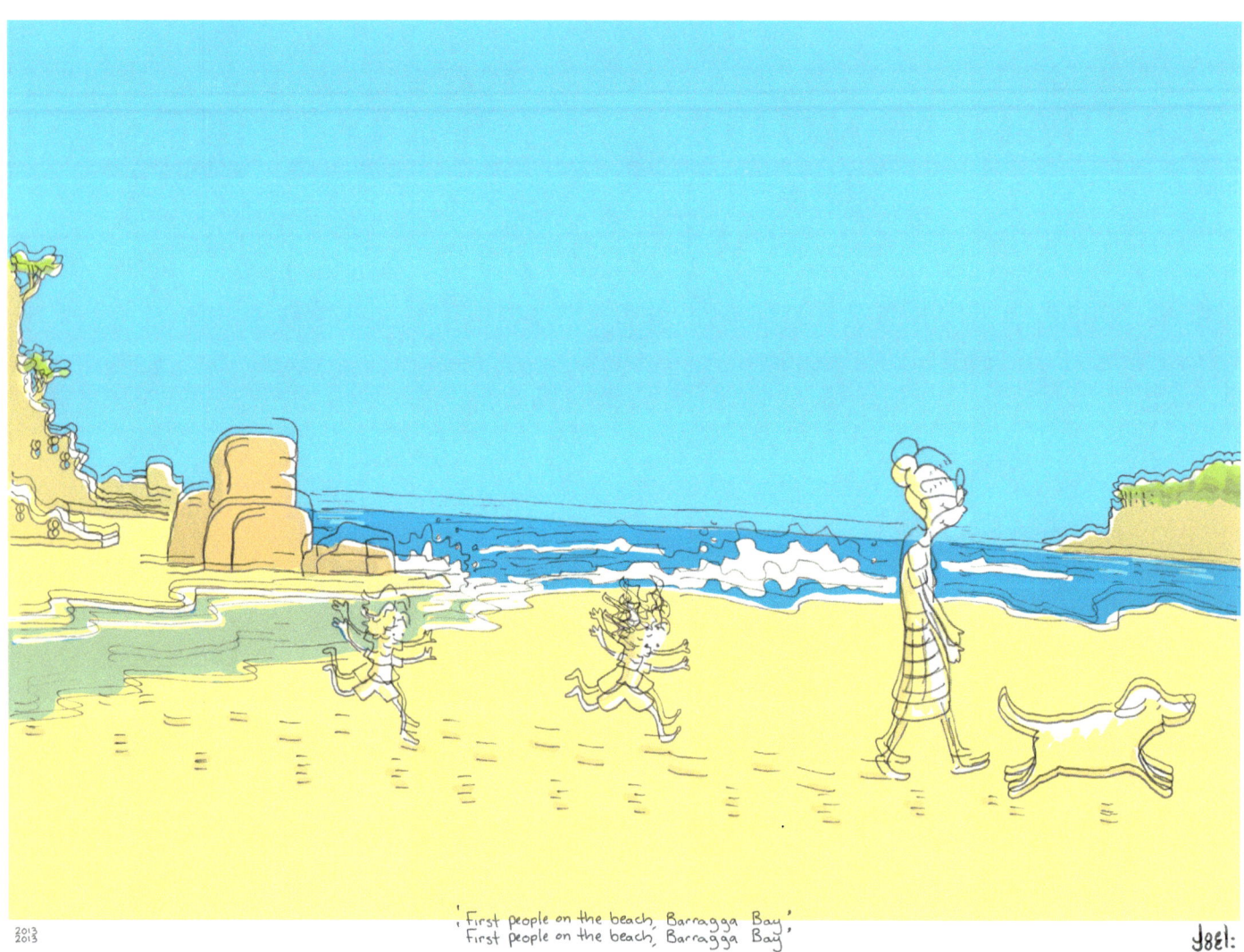

'First people on the beach, Barragga Bay'

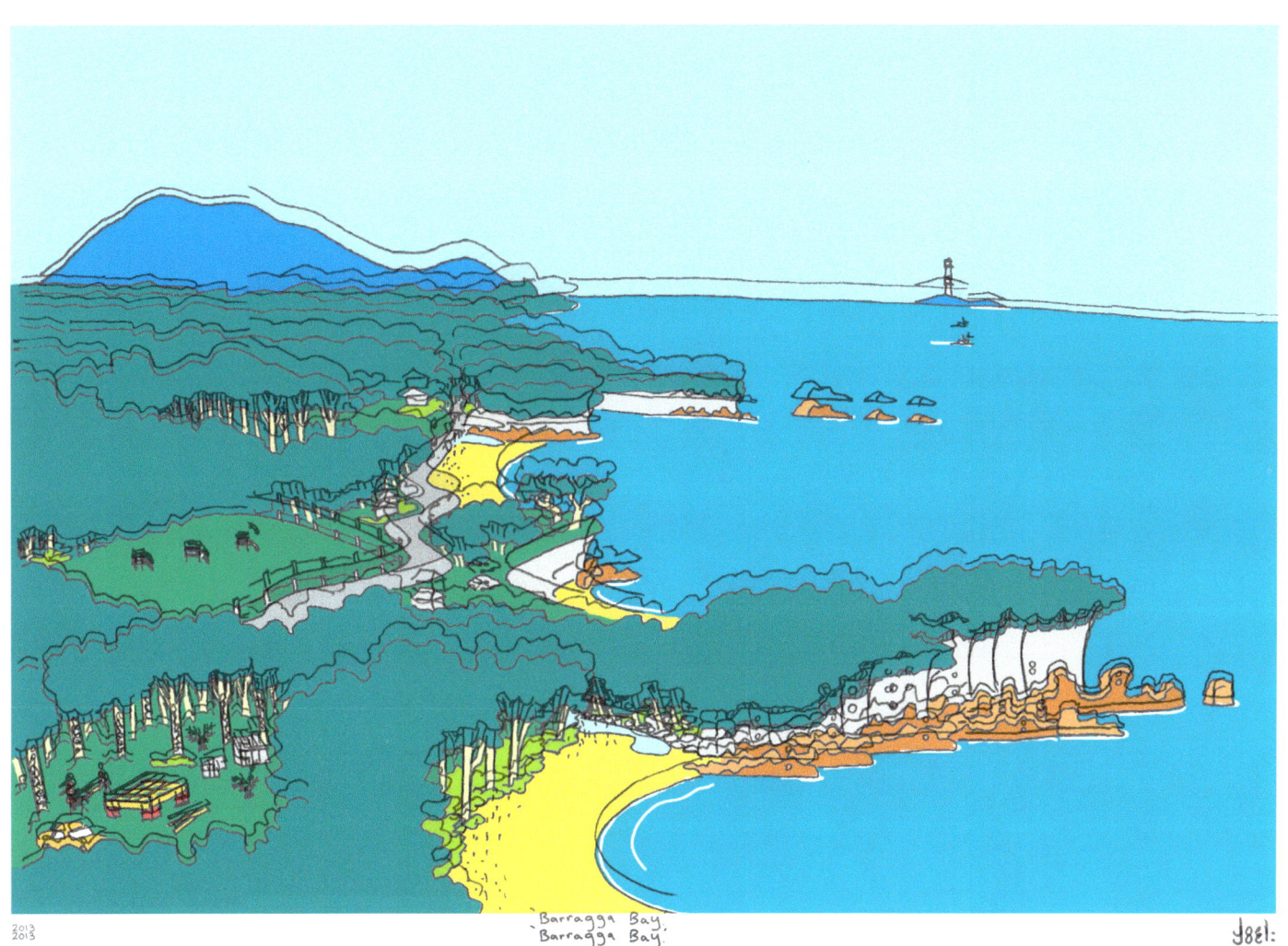

'Barragga Bay, Barragga Bay'

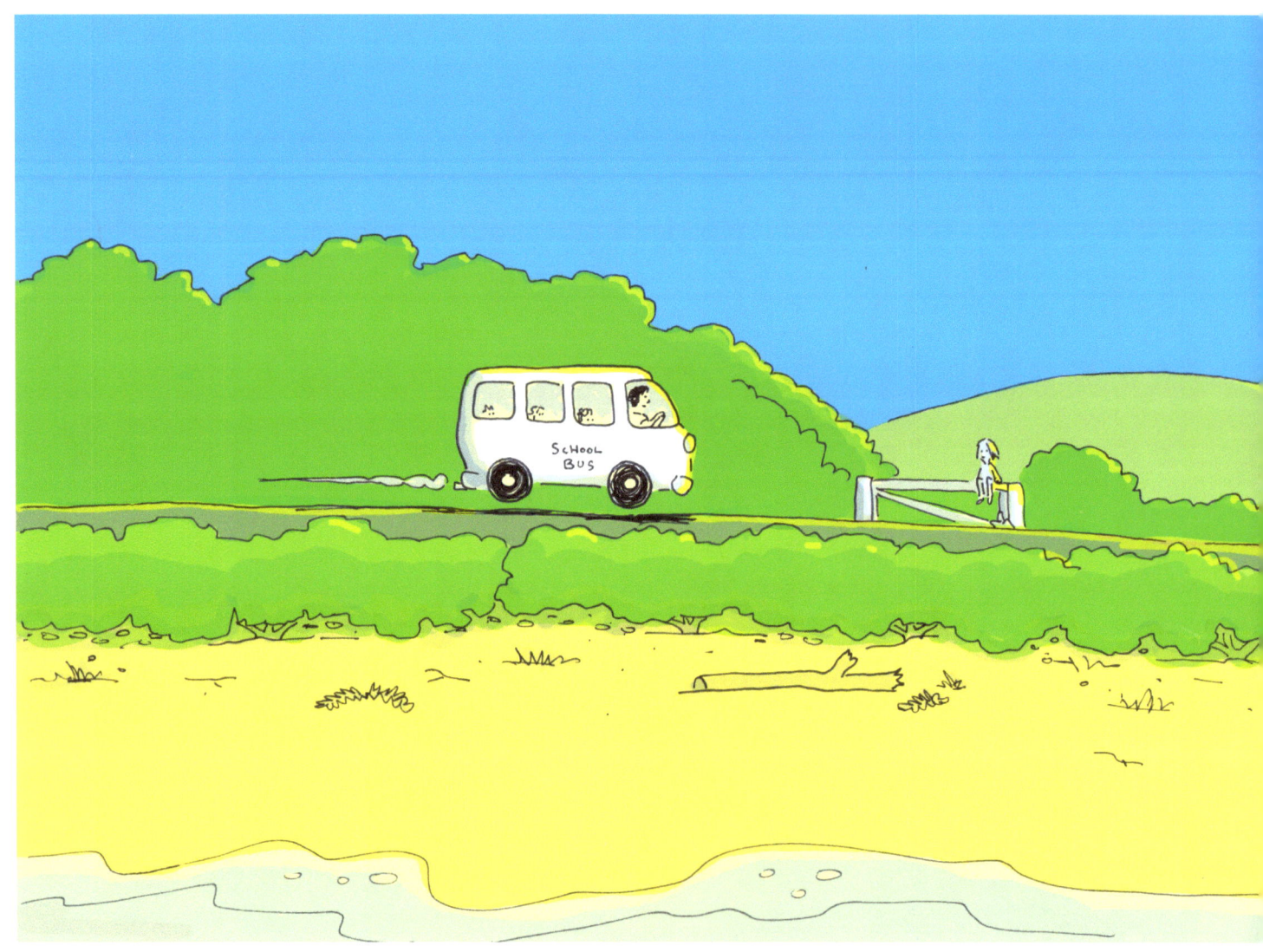

2013 'Mrs Hunter's school bus, Cuttagee'

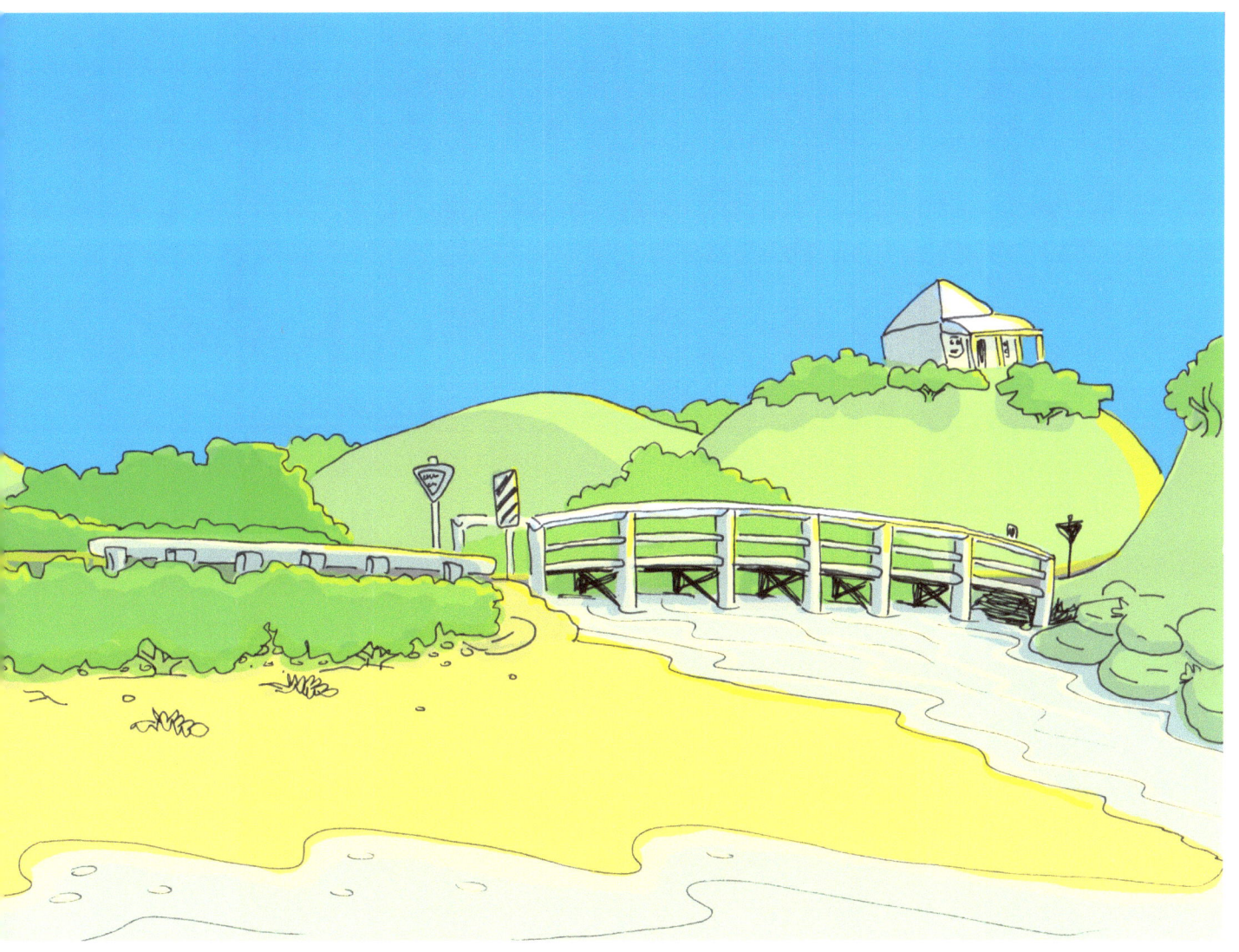

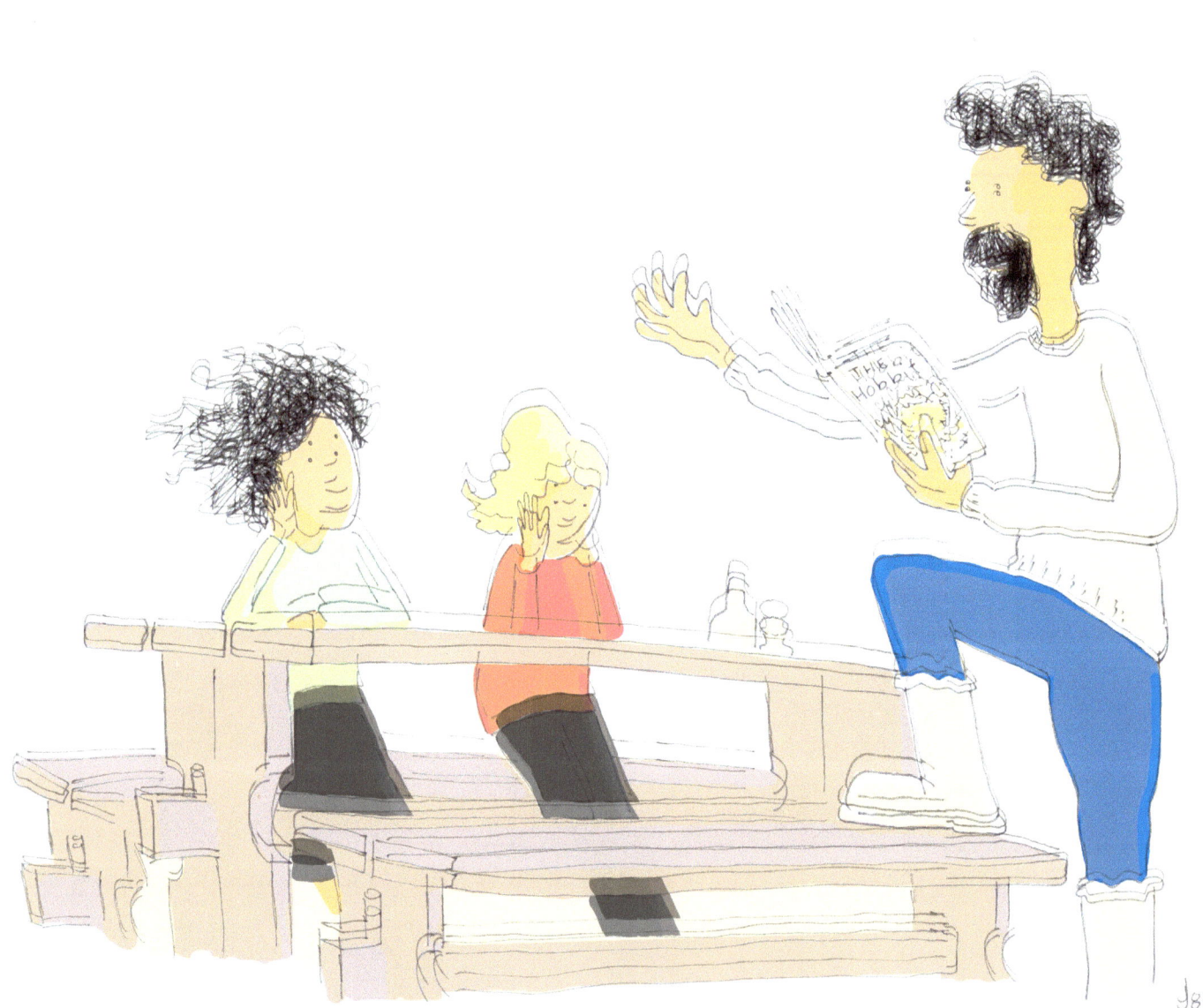

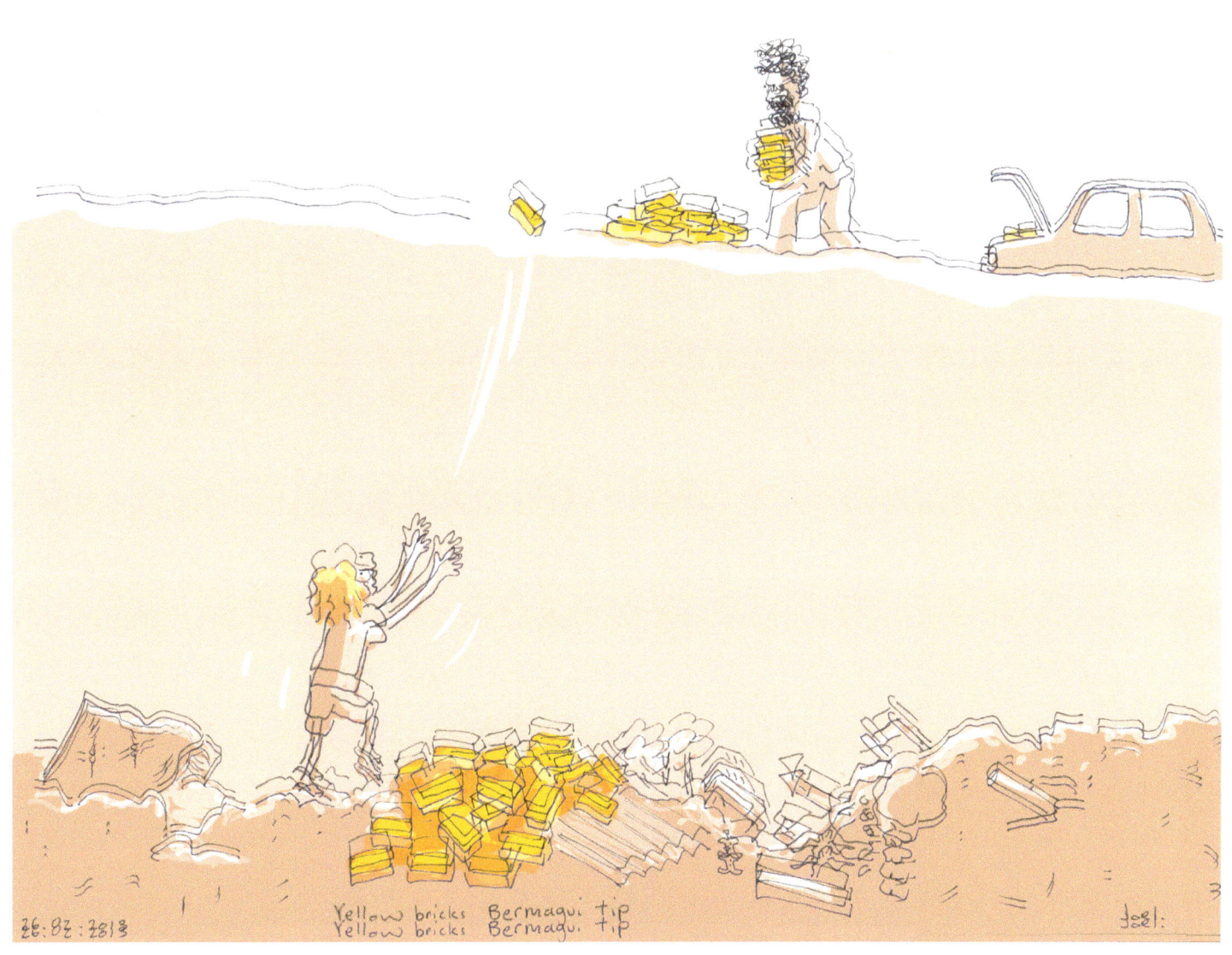

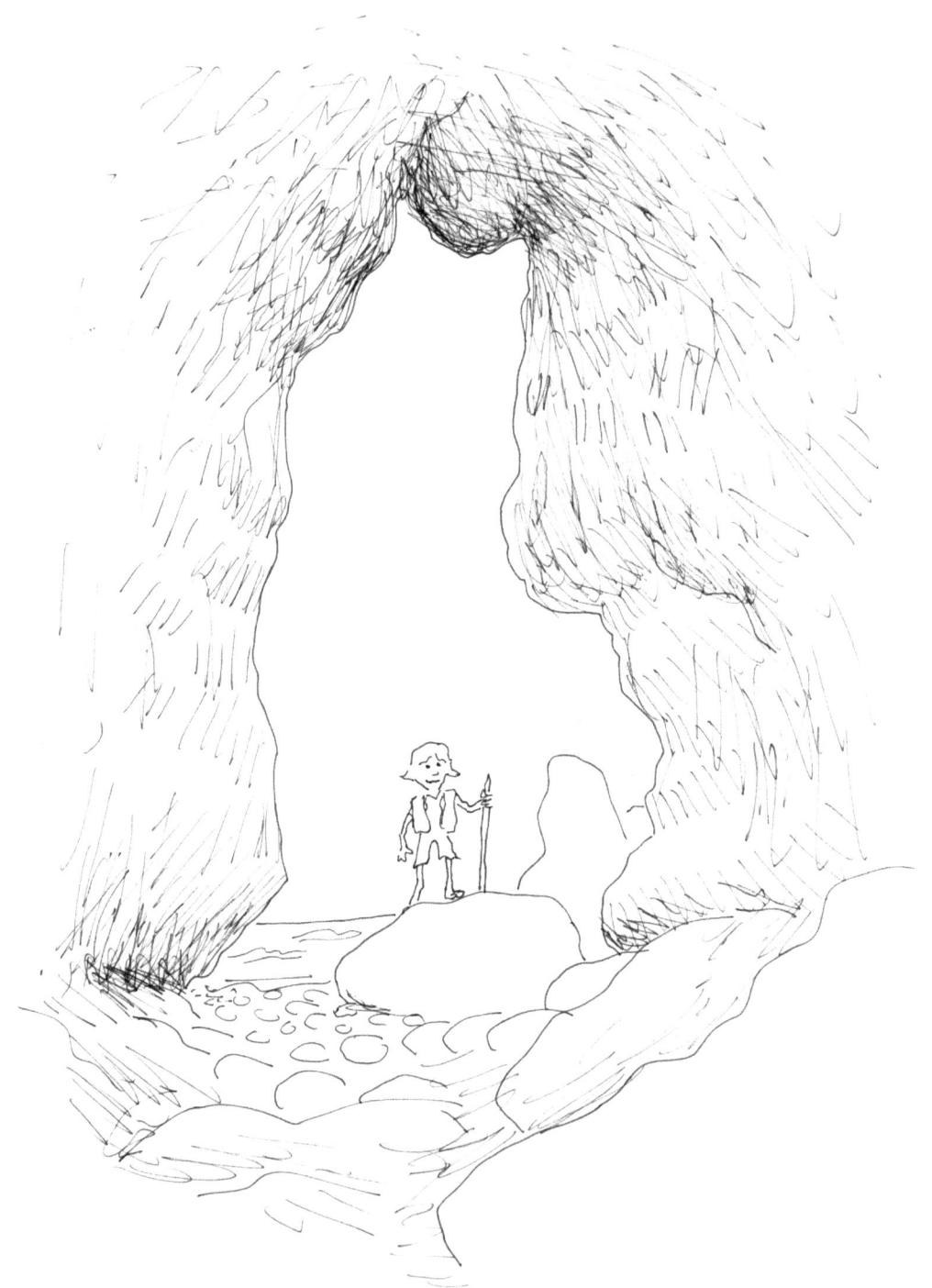

22.04.13 the sea cave Joel.

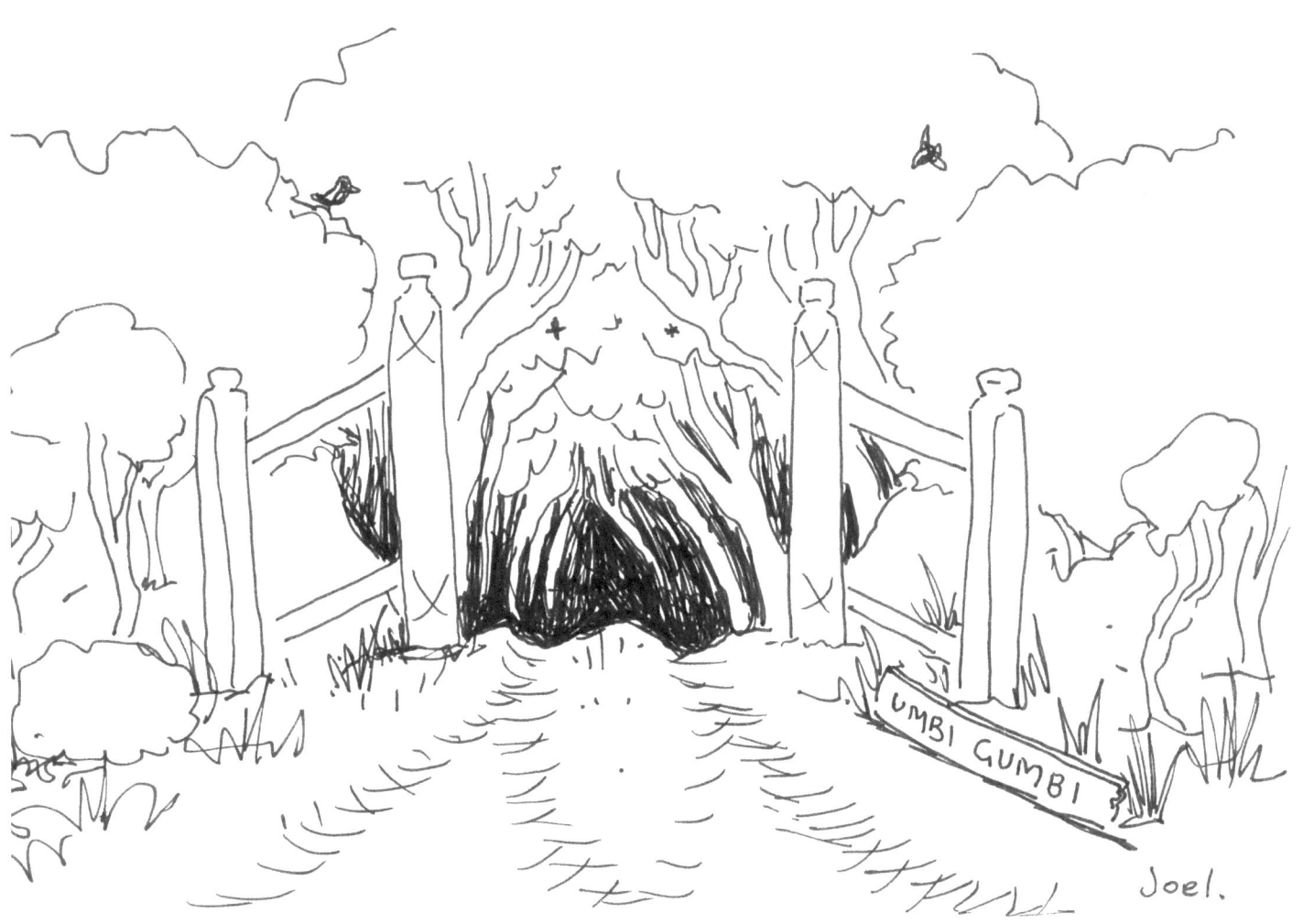

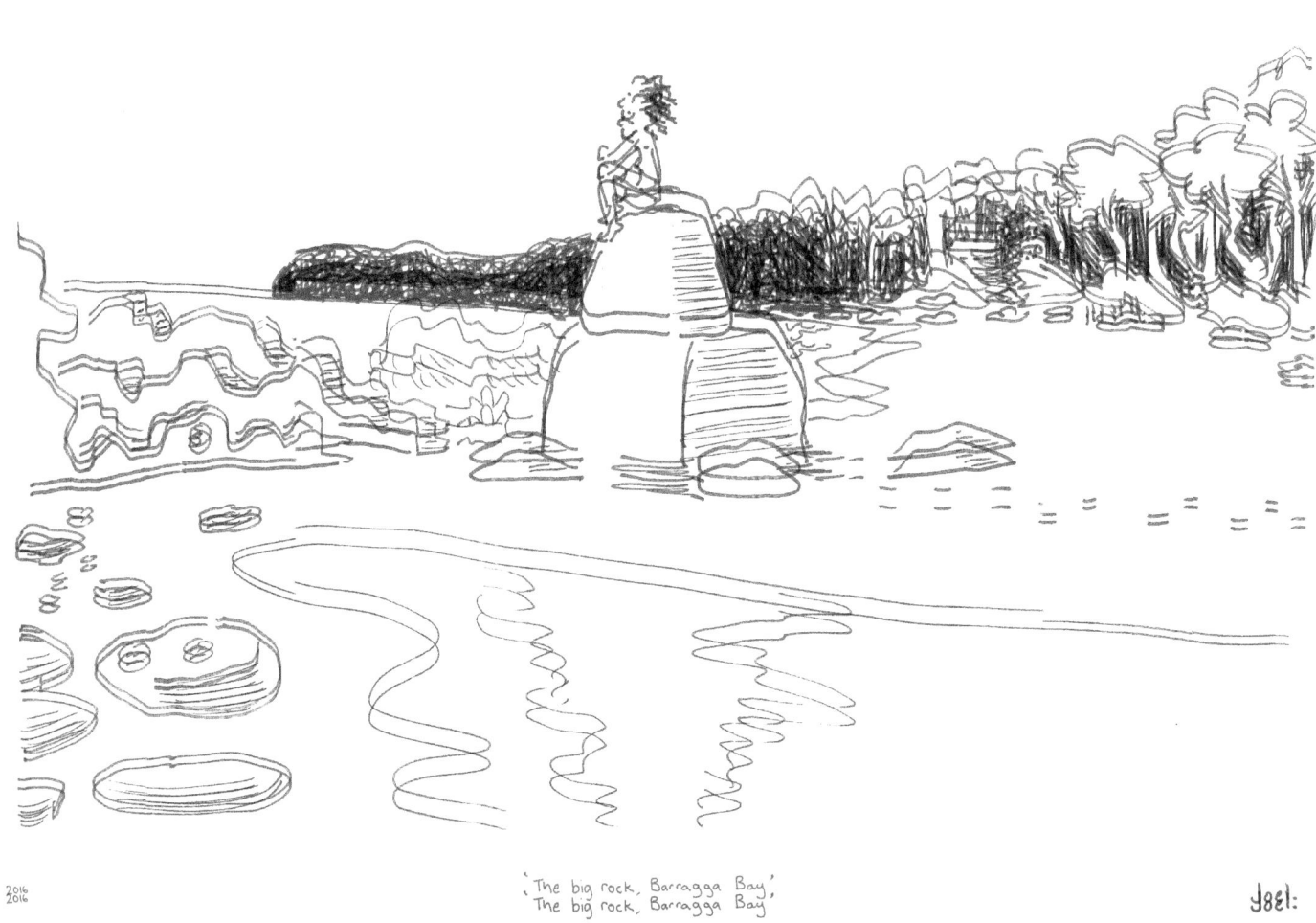

'The big rock, Barragga Bay'
The big rock, Barragga Bay

Joel Tarling

Joel completed his fine arts Diploma in 1996 at Meadowbank Tafe and has held several highly successful art exhibitions up and down the eastern seaboard of NSW.

Joel Tarling spent five years as an editorial cartoonist for The Sydney City Hub 2004-2008 where his work also featured in The Green Weekly, The Big Issue and AVANT card. He has also illustrated for Sydney Water, Sydney University, 33 Creative, Koori Curriculum, Wave Consulting, Inner West Council, Blacktown Council, The Environmental Protection Agency, Federation Press, Social Change Media, Frenzal Rhomb, Trout Fishing In Quebec, Old Spice Boys, Mr. Conway and various other bands. At high school he did work experience with artist Martin Sharp and wrote a series of undergound comics.

www.joeltarling.com
@joeltarling

www.redbubble.com/people/joeltarling/shop

You might also like these:

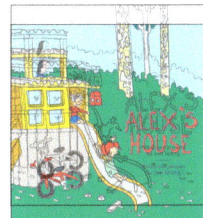

Written and illustrated by Joel Tarling
www.amazon.com.au/Alexs-House-Joel-Tarling/dp/1722190418

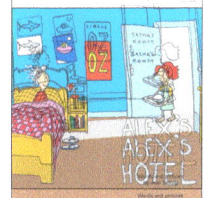

Written and illustrated by Joel Tarling
www.amazon.com/Alexs-Hotel-Mr-Joel-Tarling/dp/B09GJS714R

www.ingramcontent.com/pod-product-compliance
Lightning Source LLC
Chambersburg PA
CBHW051939210526
45473CB00006B/2311